C000212534

CLASSICAL GUITAR FAVORITES

With Tablature

Transcribed, Arranged and Edited by
David Nadal

DOVER PUBLICATIONS, INC.
Mineola, New York

Copyright

Copyright © 2004 by David Nadal and Kithara Editions
All rights reserved.

Bibliographical Note

Classical Guitar Favorites with Tablature is a new work, first published by Dover Publications, Inc., in 2004. These transcriptions, arrangements, and editions have been specially prepared for this publication.

International Standard Book Number: 0-486-43960-7

Manufactured in the United States of America
Dover Publications, Inc., 31 East 2nd Street, Mineola, N.Y. 11501

INTRODUCTION

Guitarists are a varied group of individuals. We come to our instrument for many different reasons: to accompany ourselves singing; to play a rock song we've heard on the radio; to play bossa nova, bluegrass, or Bach. Despite this diversity, we share a common curiosity that encourages us to explore the many other types of music that make up the world of guitar.

Classical Guitar Favorites with Tablature celebrates our curiosity by making available a full sampling of classical guitar solos, many of which are appearing in print for the first time. A wide range of styles and eras are represented in this compendium of pieces that have stood the test of time. Included are:

- Music of the Renaissance vihuelists and lutenists (Narvaez, Dowland and the anonymously penned *Greensleeves*).
- Music of the Baroque guitar (Visee and Guerau) and lute (Kellner).
- New transcriptions of music by late Baroque masters (Bach and Scarlatti).
- Works of the early 19th-century guitar masters (Sor, Giuliani and Aguado) along with one of the seldom-performed guitar works of the eminent violinist Paganini.
- An intimate *Prelude* by Chopin, perfectly suited for the guitar.
- Music of the late 19th-century Spanish nationalist composers, as represented by Albeniz's *Asturias* (which, it is sometimes forgotten, was originally written for piano).
- A new arrangement of Satie's *Gnossienne No. 1* (also originally for piano).
- The well-known serenade *Capricho Árabe*, by the father of modern classical guitar, Francisco Tárrega.

I have included guitar tablature so that those who are less fluent in reading standard music notation may also have access to this rich heritage of music. I hope that this collection brings you as much joy as I have had in preparing it.

DAVID NADAL
Queens, NY
Summer 2004

A native of New York City, David Nadal is a performer on both the classical and electric guitar. He has performed at the Other Minds Festival in San Francisco, the New York Guitar Festival, the Norfolk Chamber Music Festival, Roulette and the Knitting Factory. An expert on the classical guitar literature, Mr. Nadal has published over five volumes of his critically acclaimed transcriptions and arrangements with Dover Publications. Recently, he was guitar coach to Peter Sarsgaard for the FoxSearchlight feature film, "Garden State." He is a founding member of the Sap Dream Electric Guitar Quartet, and has taught at the Juilliard School's Pre-College Division and the Choir Academy of Harlem. Currently, David is a member of the faculty at LaGuardia Community College (CUNY) and the Amadeus Conservatory in Chappaqua, NY. David has earned degrees in classical guitar performance from both Manhattan School of Music and Yale University. He lives in Elmhurst, Queens, New York where he also maintains an active guitar studio.

TABLE OF CONTENTS

LUYS DE NARVÁEZ	Guardame las Vacas	2
JOHN DOWLAND	The Frog Galliard	4
	Fantasie	7
ROBERT DE VISÉE	Suite in D minor	
	I. Prelude	13
	II. Allemande	14
	III. Courante	16
	IV. Sarabande	17
	V. Gavotte	18
	VI. Minuet I	19
	VII. Minuet II	20
	VIII. Bourrée	21
	IX. Gigue	22
FRANCISCO GUERAU	Marionas	24
	Canario	28
ANONYMOUS	Greensleeves	31
DOMENICO SCARLATTI	Sonata in A, K209	32
	Sonata in A, K322	38
DAVID KELLNER	Phantasia in D minor	42
JOHANN SEBASTIAN BACH	Prelude	46
	Gavotte I and II	50
MAURO GIULIANI	Sonatine, Op. 71, No. 1	
	I. Maestoso	54
	II. Minuetto	58
	III. Rondo	61
DIONISIO AGUADO	Study in A minor	65
MAURO GIULIANI	Allegro, Op. 100, No. 1	66
	Study in F, Op. 51, No. 13	70
	Study in D, Op. 50, No. 25	72
FERNANDO SOR	Study in C, Op. 31, No. 4	74
	Study in A, Op. 6, No. 2	75
	Study in A minor, Op. 31, No. 20	76
	Study in D, Op. 35, No. 17	78
	Study in B♭, Op. 29, No. 13	80
	Grand Solo, Op. 14	84
NICOLÒ PAGANINI	Sonata No. 26	
	I. Minuetto per la Signora Marina	99
	II. Allegretto	100
FRÉDÉRIC CHOPIN	Prelude, Op. 28, No. 7	102
ISAAC ALBÉNIZ	Asturias (Leyenda), Op. 47/232	103
ERIK SATIE	Gnossienne No. 1	112
FRANCISCO TÁRREGA	Capricho Árabe	116

Index by Composer

Aguado, Dionisio (1784–1849)
    Study in A minor   65

Albéniz, Isaac (1860–1909)
    Asturias (Leyenda), Op. 47/232   103

Anonymous (16th century)
    Greensleeves   31

Bach, Johann Sebastian (1685–1750)
    Prelude   46
    Gavotte I and II   50

Chopin, Frédéric (1809–1840)
    Prelude, Op. 28, No. 7   102

Dowland, John (1563–1626)
    The Frog Galliard   4
    Fantasie   7

Giuliani, Mauro (1781–1829)
    Sonatine, Op. 71, No. 1   54
    Allegro, Op. 100, No. 1   66
    Study in F, Op. 51, No. 13   70
    Study in D, Op. 50, No. 25   72

Guerau, Francisco (1649–1722)
    Marionas   24
    Canario   28

Kellner, David (c. 1670–1748)
    Phantasia in D minor   42

Narváez, Luys de (fl. 1530–1550)
    Guardame las Vacas   2

Paganini, Nicolò (1782–1840)
    Sonata No. 26   99

Satie, Erik (1866–1925)
    Gnossienne No. 1   112

Scarlatti, Domenico (1685–1757)
    Sonata in A, K209   32
    Sonata in A, K322   38

Sor, Fernando (1778–1839)
    Study in C, Op. 31, No. 4   74
    Study in A, Op. 6, No. 2   75
    Study in A minor, Op. 31, No. 20   76
    Study in D, Op. 35, No. 17   78
    Study in B♭, Op. 29, No. 13   80
    Grand Solo, Op. 14   84

Tárrega, Francisco (1852–1909)
    Capricho Árabe   116

Visée, Robert de (c. 1655–c. 1732)
    Suite in D minor   13

Glossary of Guitar Notation

Strings:

- ①—1st string E
- ②—2nd string B
- ③—3rd string G
- ④—4th string D
- ⑤—5th string A
- ⑥—6th string E

Left Hand:

- 1—index finger
- 2—middle finger
- 3—ring finger
- 4—pinky finger
- 0—open string

Right Hand:

- *p*—thumb
- *i*—index finger
- *m*—middle finger
- *a*—ring finger

Tablature: A six line staff that graphically represents the guitar fingerboard.

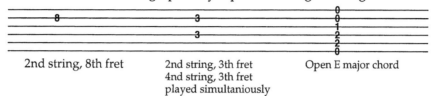

2nd string, 8th fret   2nd string, 3th fret   Open E major chord
                            4nd string, 3th fret
                            played simultaniously

Three string **barré**   Six string **barré**
in the 2nd position.   in the 3rd position.

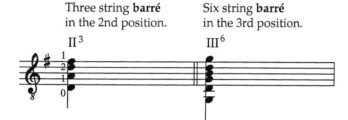

Ascending slur or   **Descending slur** or
"Hammer–on"   *"Pull–off"*

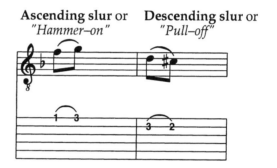

Natural Harmonic:
Lightly touch the string
over the indicated fret and
pluck with the right hand.

Natural Harmonic

Artificial Harmonic:
Fret note one octave below
indicated pitch and lightly touch
the fret 12 frets above it on the same
string while plucking with *a* or *p*.

Artificial Harmonic or
R.H. Harmonic

Ornaments:

is played   is played   is played

CLASSICAL GUITAR FAVORITES
With Tablature

Guardame las Vacas

from *Los Seys Libros del Delphín*

Luys de Narváez
(*fl.* 1530–1550)

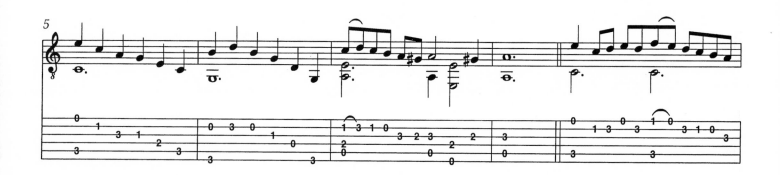

The Frog Galliard

from *The Dowland Lute Book*

John Dowland
(1563–1626)

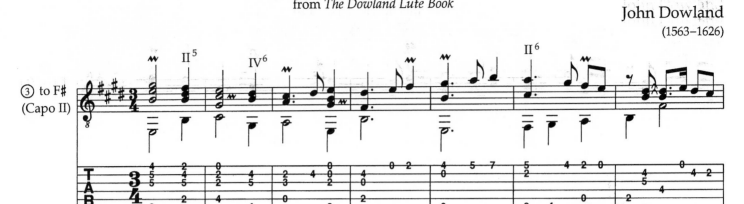

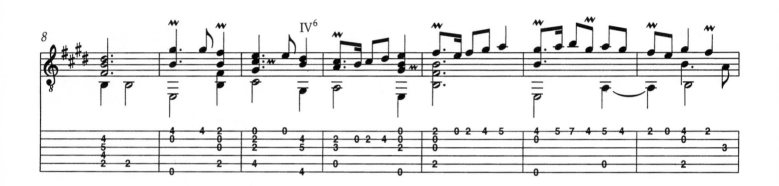

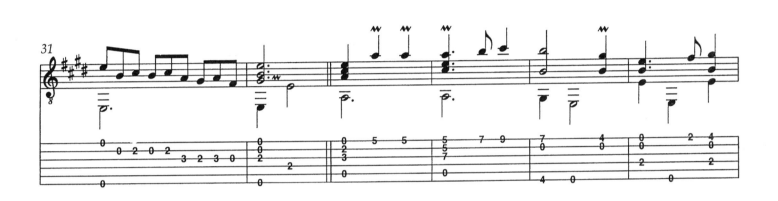

Fantasie

from *A Varietie of Lute Lessons*

John Dowland
(1563–1626)

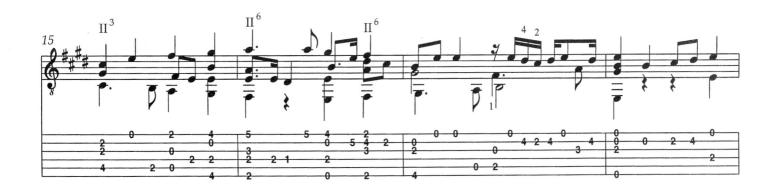

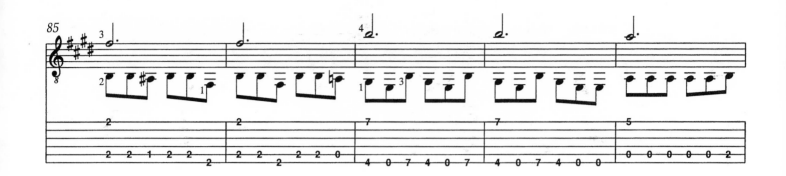

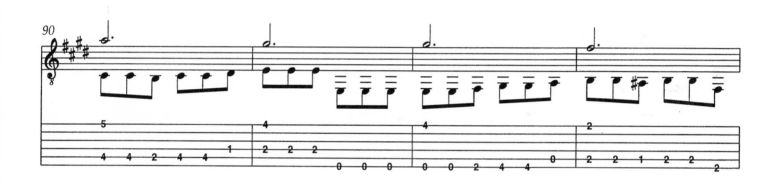

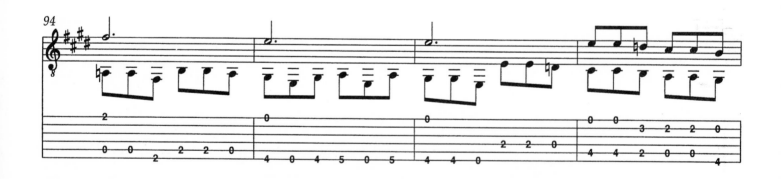

Suite in D minor

from *Livre de Pièces Pour la Guitarre*

Robert de Visée
(c. 1655–c. 1732)

[Somewhat freely]   I. Prelude

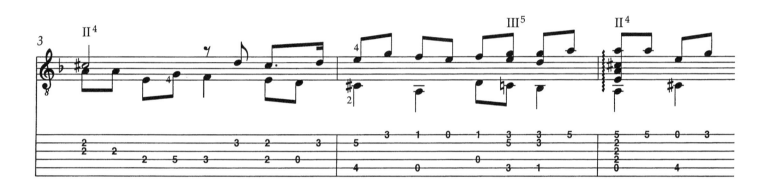

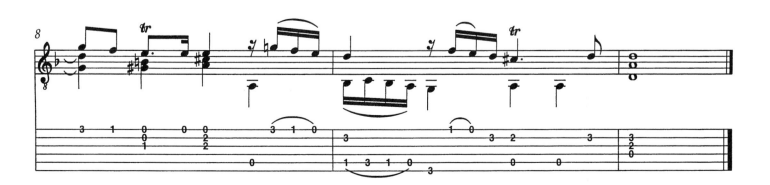

II. Allemande

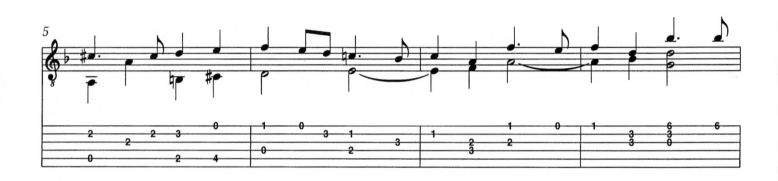

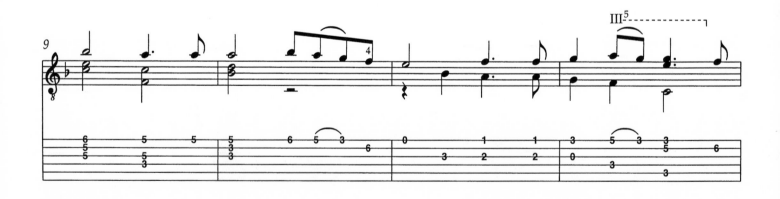

III. Courante

IV. Sarabande

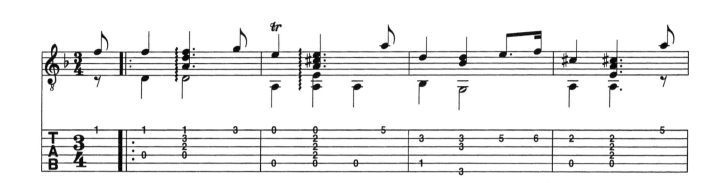

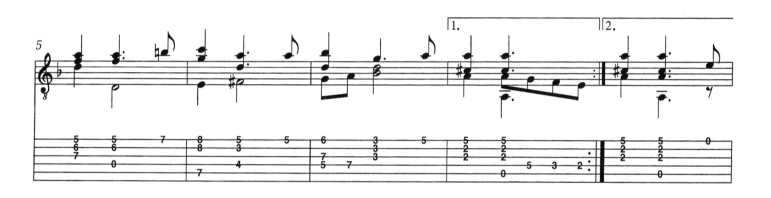

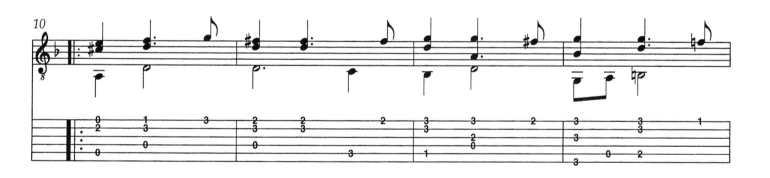

V. Gavotte

VI. Minuet I

VII. Minuet II

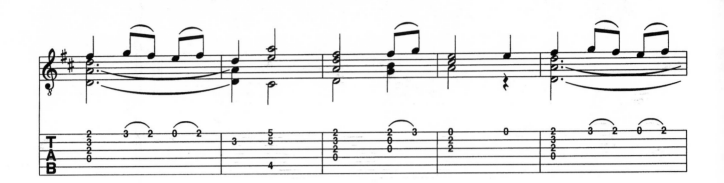

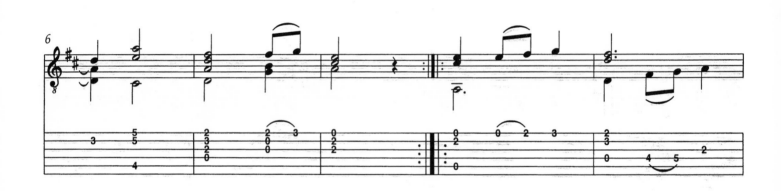

Minuet I da Capo

VIII. Bourrée

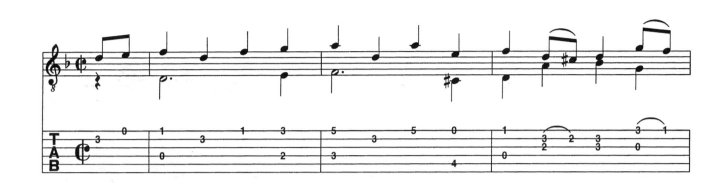

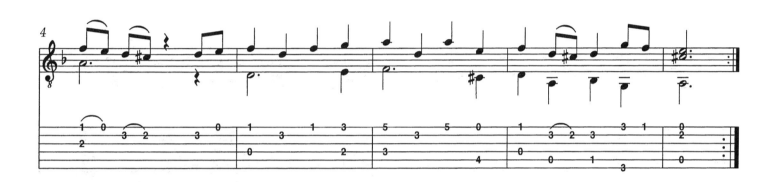

IX. Gigue

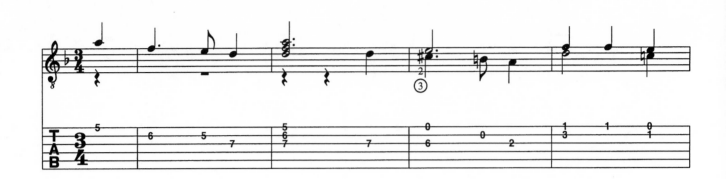

Marionas

from *Poema Harmónico*

Francisco Guerau
(1649–1722)

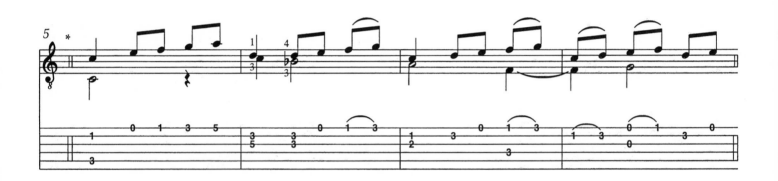

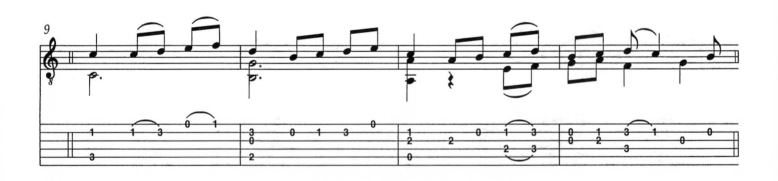

*) The performer may treat these bar lines as repeats if he or she wishes.

26

Canario

from *Poema Harmónico*

Francisco Guerau

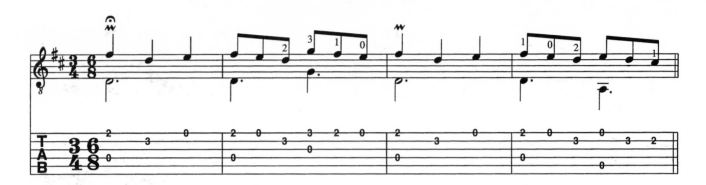

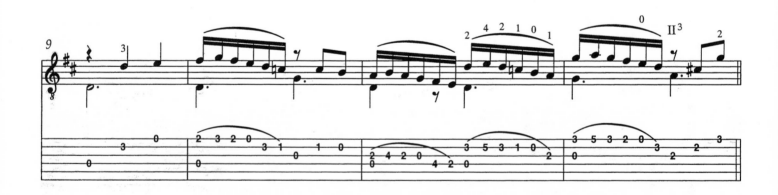

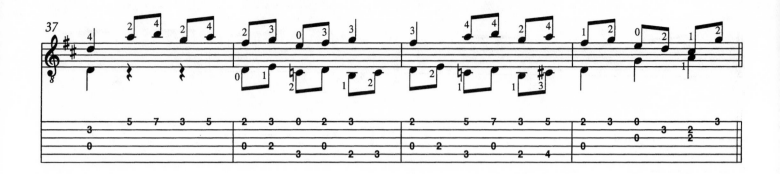

Greensleeves

Anonymous
(16th Century)

Sonata in A

K209

Domenico Scarlatti
(1685–1757)

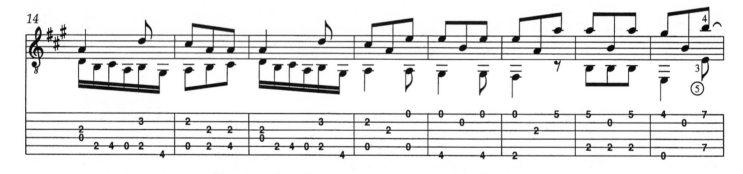

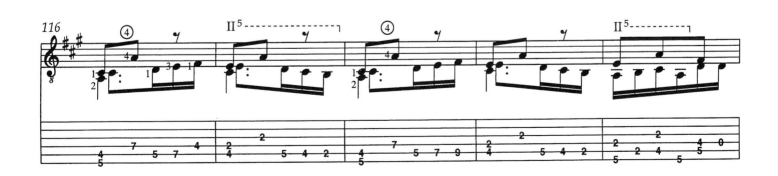

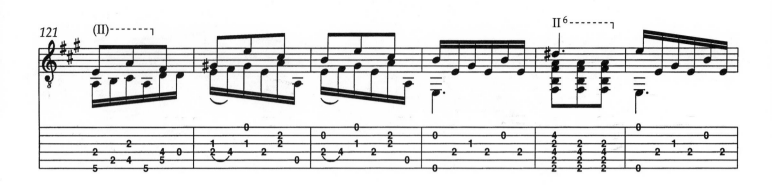

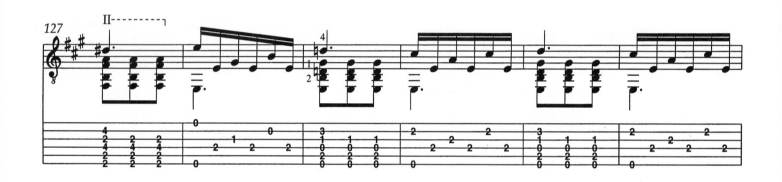

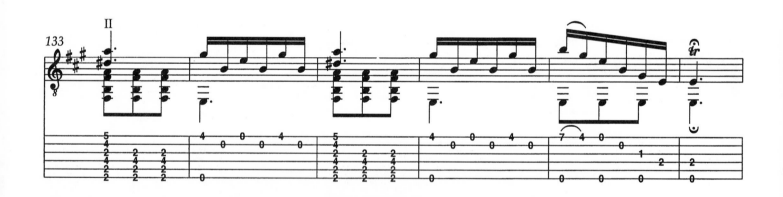

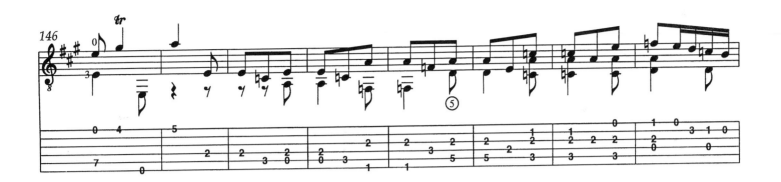

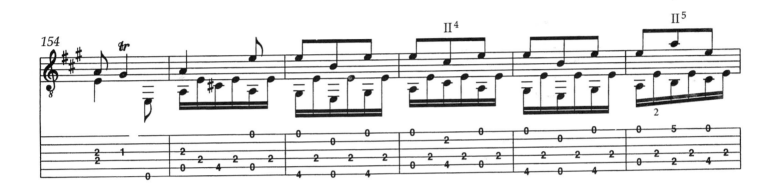

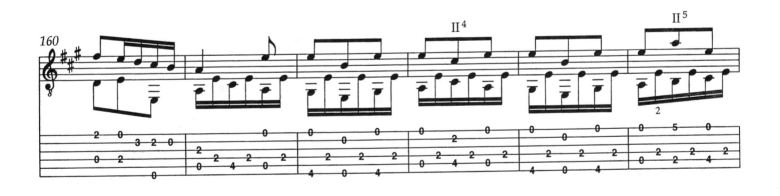

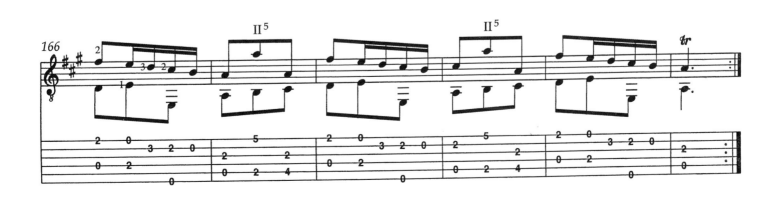

Sonata in A

K322

Domenico Scarlatti

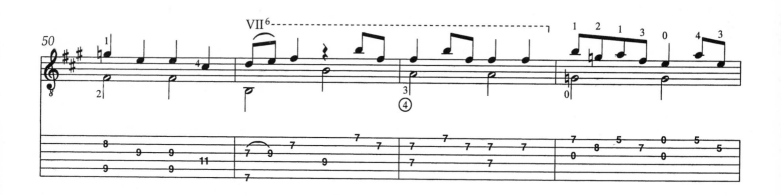

Phantasia in D minor

from *XVI Auserlesene Lauten–Stücke*

David Kellner
(*c.* 1670–1748)

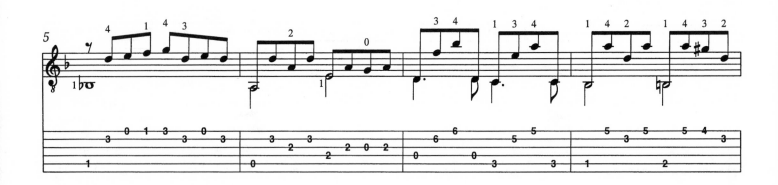

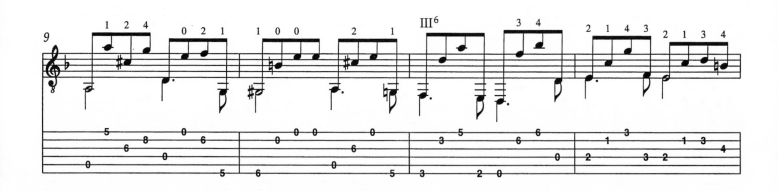

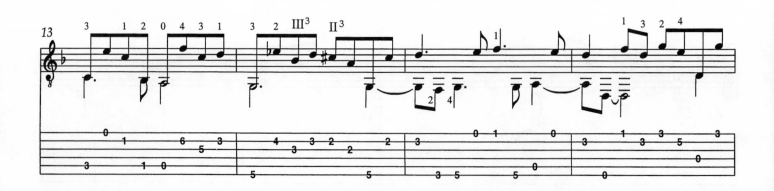

43

Prelude

from *Cello Suite No. 1 in G, BWV 1007*

Johann Sebastian Bach
(1685–1750)

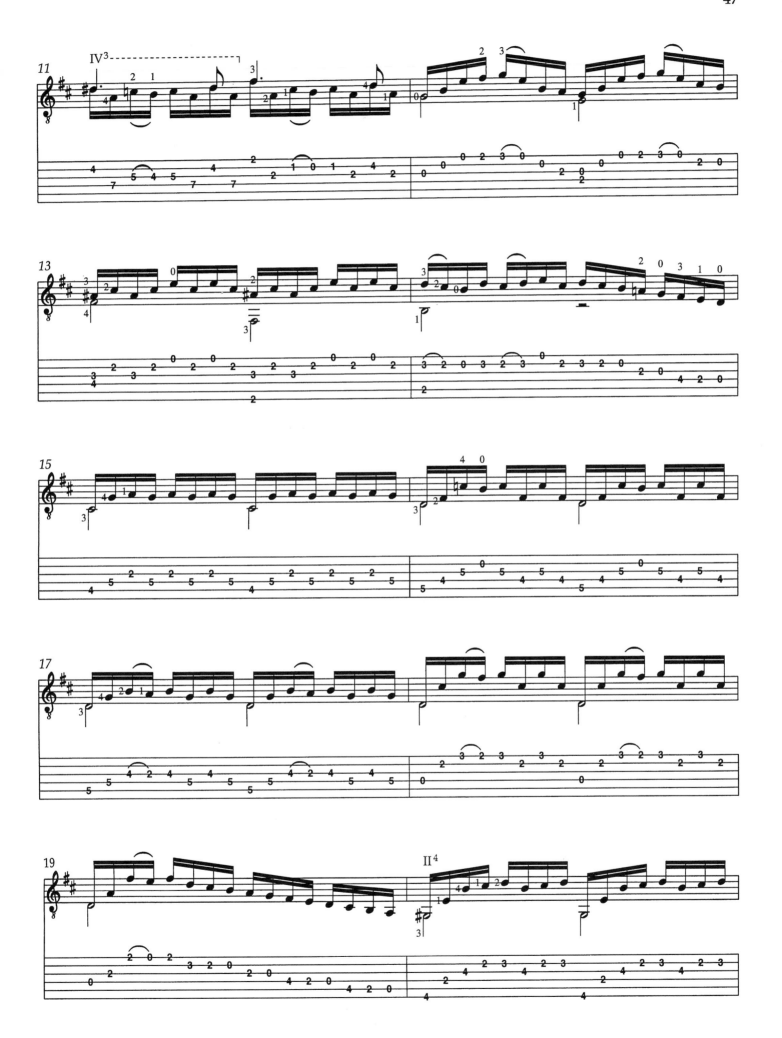

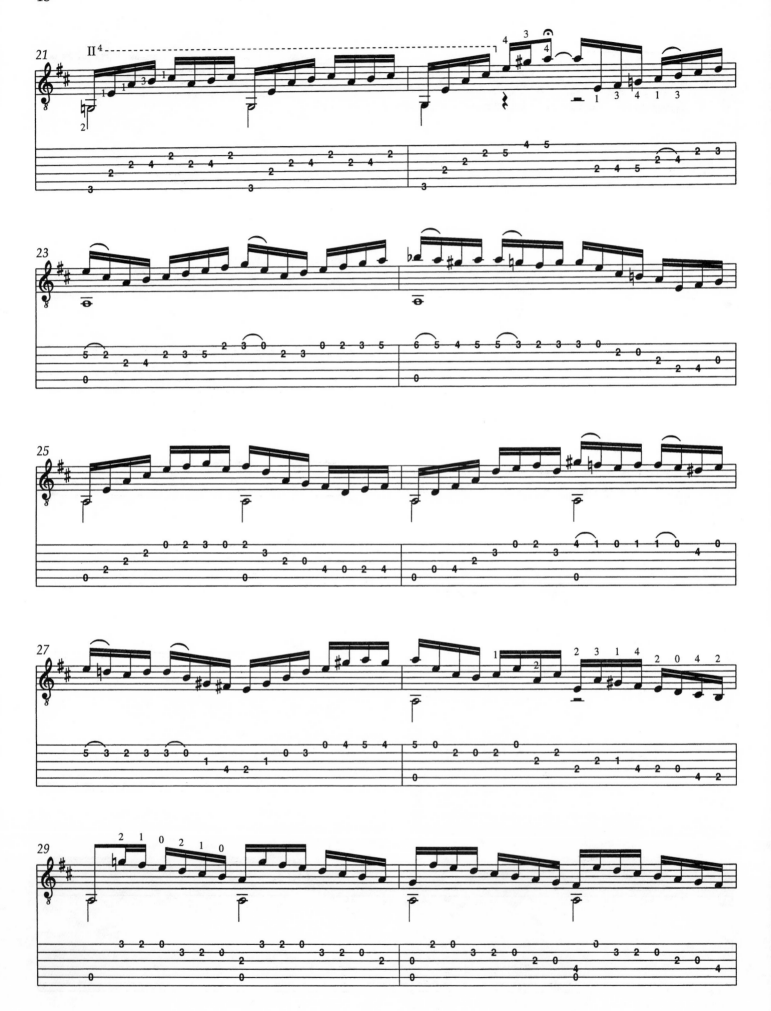

Gavotte I

from *Suite pour la Luth*, BWV 995

Johann Sebastian Bach

Gavotte II

Johann Sebastian Bach

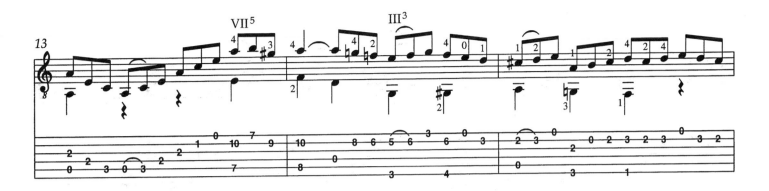

Gavotte I al Fine

Sonatine
Op. 71, No. 1

Mauro Giuliani
(1781–1829)

I. Maestoso

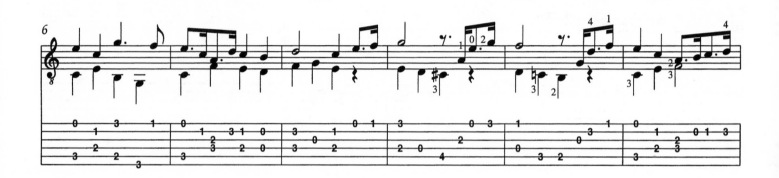

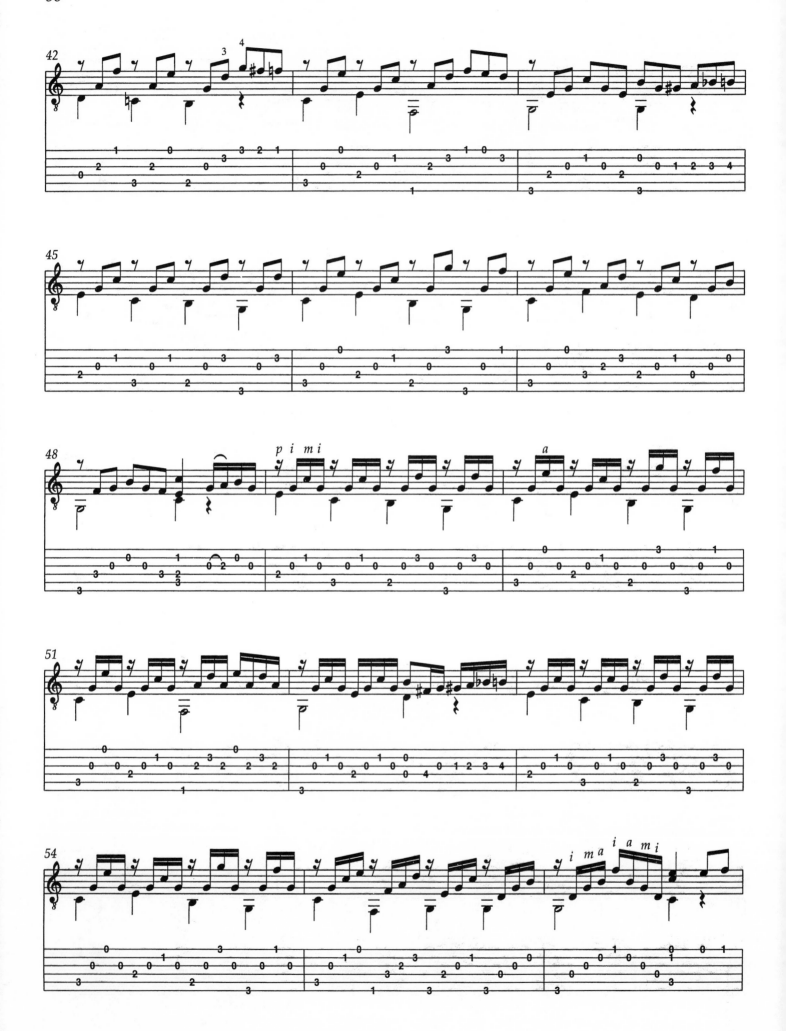

II. Minuetto

Fine

Trio

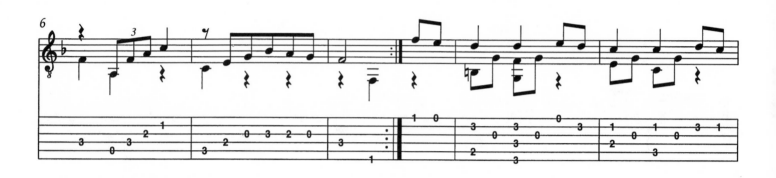

D.C. Menuetto al Fine

III. Rondo

Study in A minor

Lección 19 from *Nuevo Método para Guitarra*

Dionisio Aguado
(1784–1849)

Allegro

Op. 100, No. 1

Mauro Giuliani

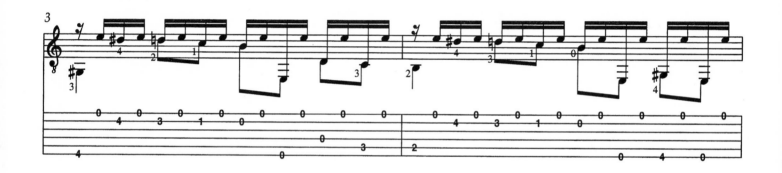

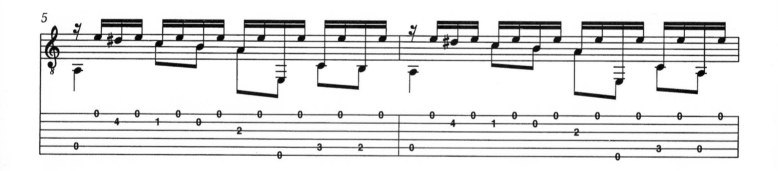

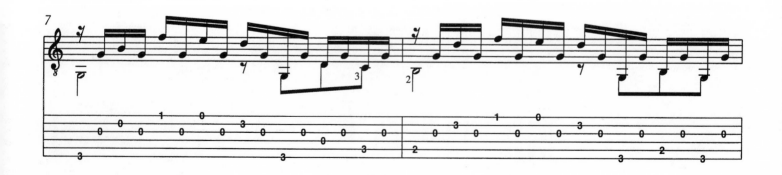

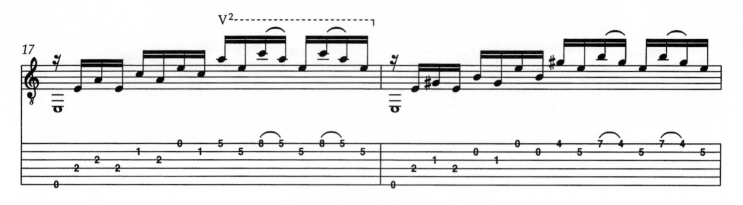

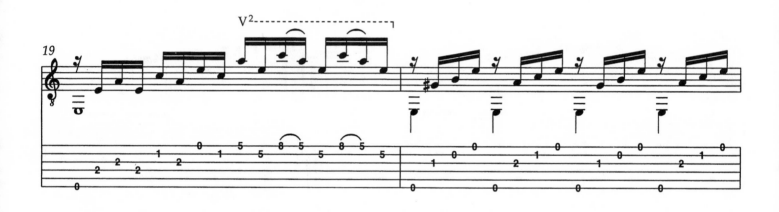

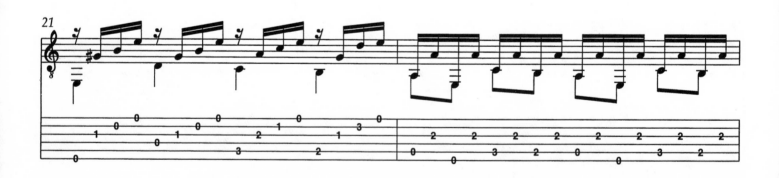

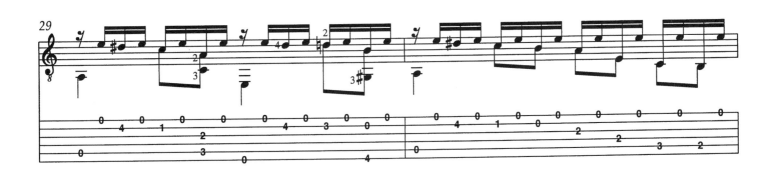

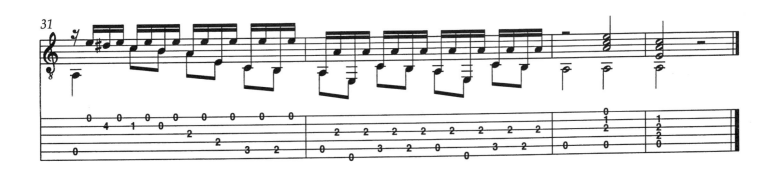

Study in F
Op. 51, No. 13

Mauro Giuliani

Study in D

Op. 50, No. 25

Mauro Giuliani

Andantino grazioso

Study in C

No. 4 from *Vingt Quatre Leçons Progressives*, Op. 31

Fernando Sor
(1778–1839)

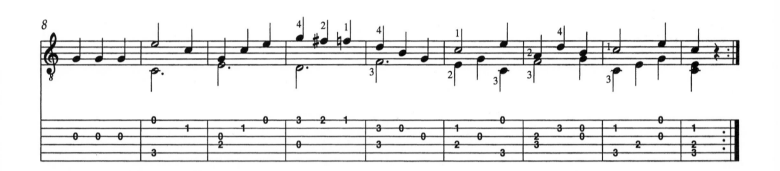

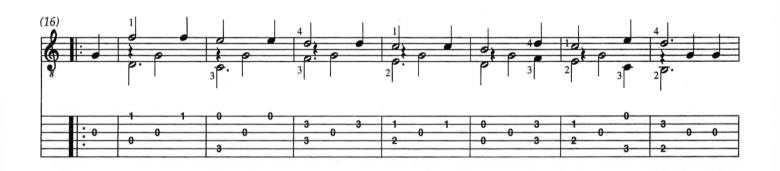

Study in A

No. 2 from *Twelve Studies*, Op. 6

Fernando Sor

Andante allegro

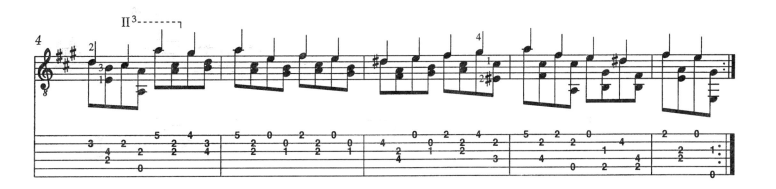

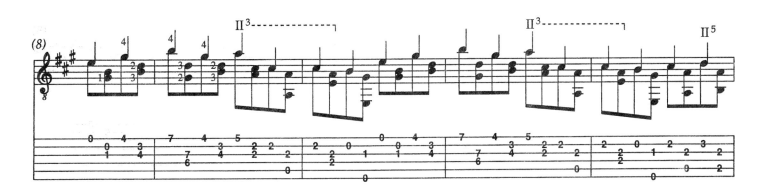

Study in A minor

No. 20 from *Vingt Quatre Leçons Progressives*, Op. 31

Fernando Sor

Andante allegro

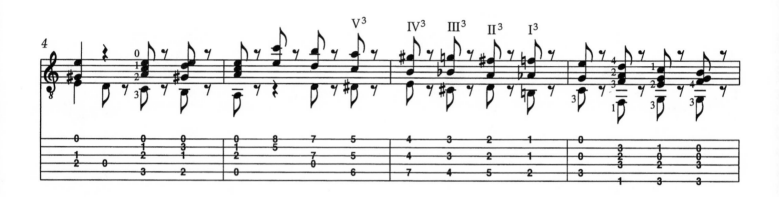

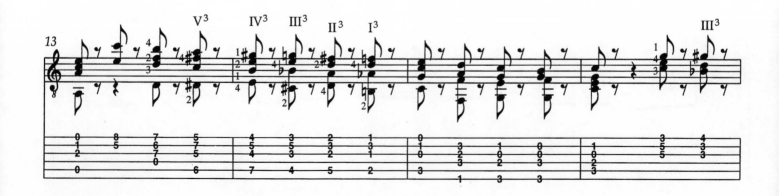

Study in D

No. 17 from *Vingt Quatre Leçons Progressives*, Op. 35

Fernando Sor

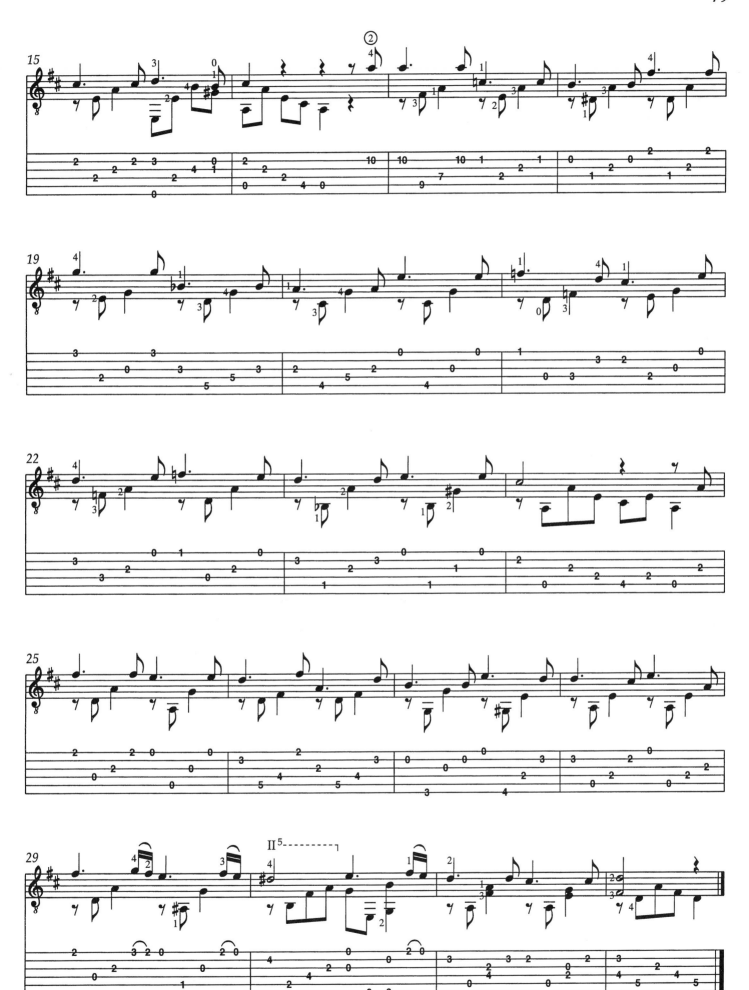

Study in B♭

No. 13 from *Twelve Studies*, Op. 29

Fernando Sor

Andante lento

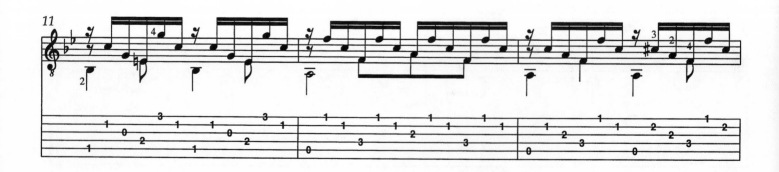

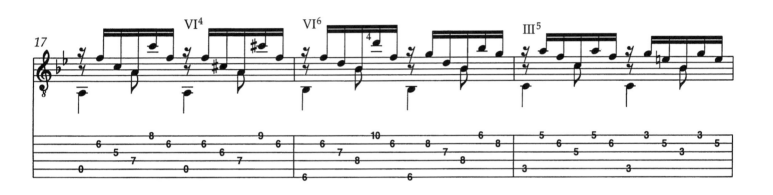

Grand Solo

Op. 14

Fernando Sor

94

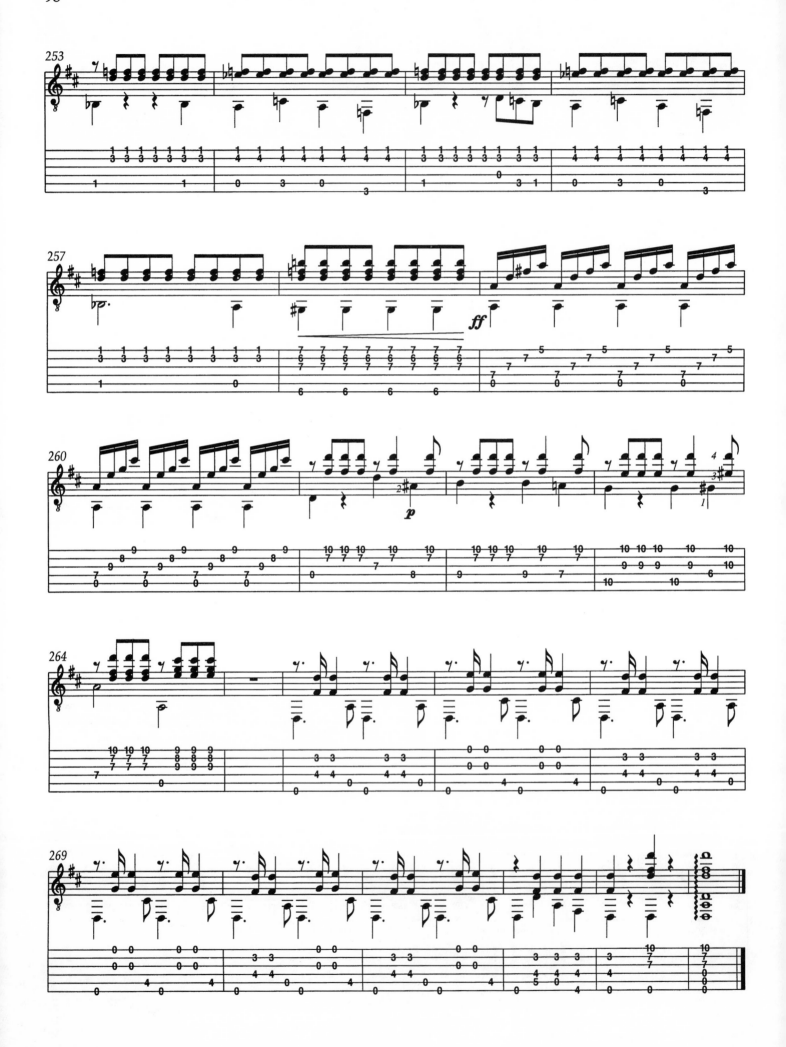

Sonata No. 26

I. Minuetto per la Signora Marina

Nicolò Paganini
(1782–1840)

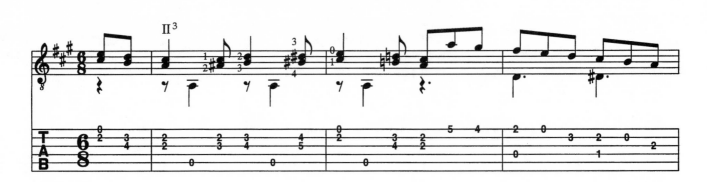

II. Allegretto

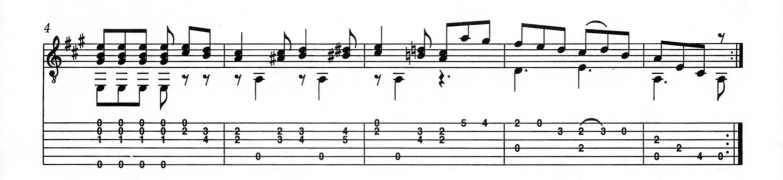

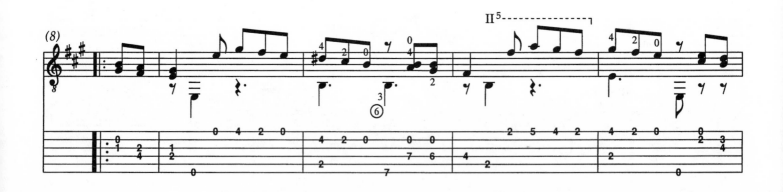

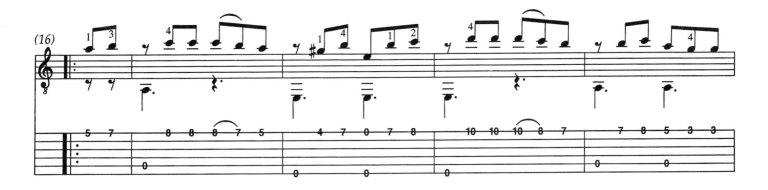

D.C. al Fine

Prelude

No. 7 from *Twenty–four Preludes*, Op. 28

Frédéric Chopin
(1809–1840)
arrangement by FRANCISCO TÁRREGA
revised by David Nadal

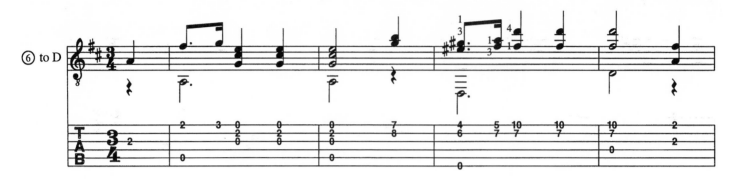

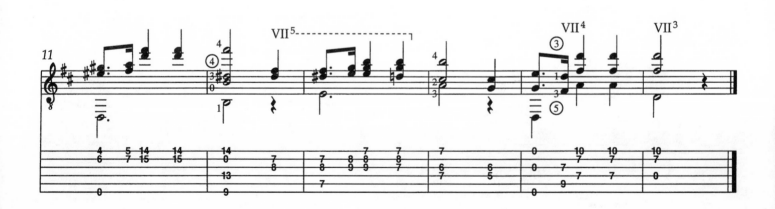

Asturias (Leyenda)

from Opp. 47/232

Isaac Albéniz
(1852–1909)

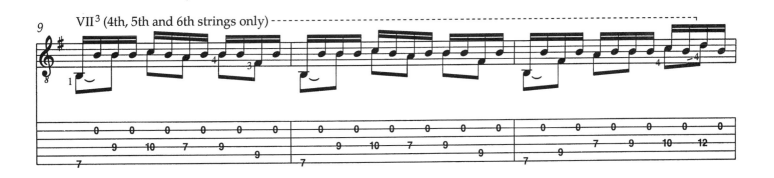

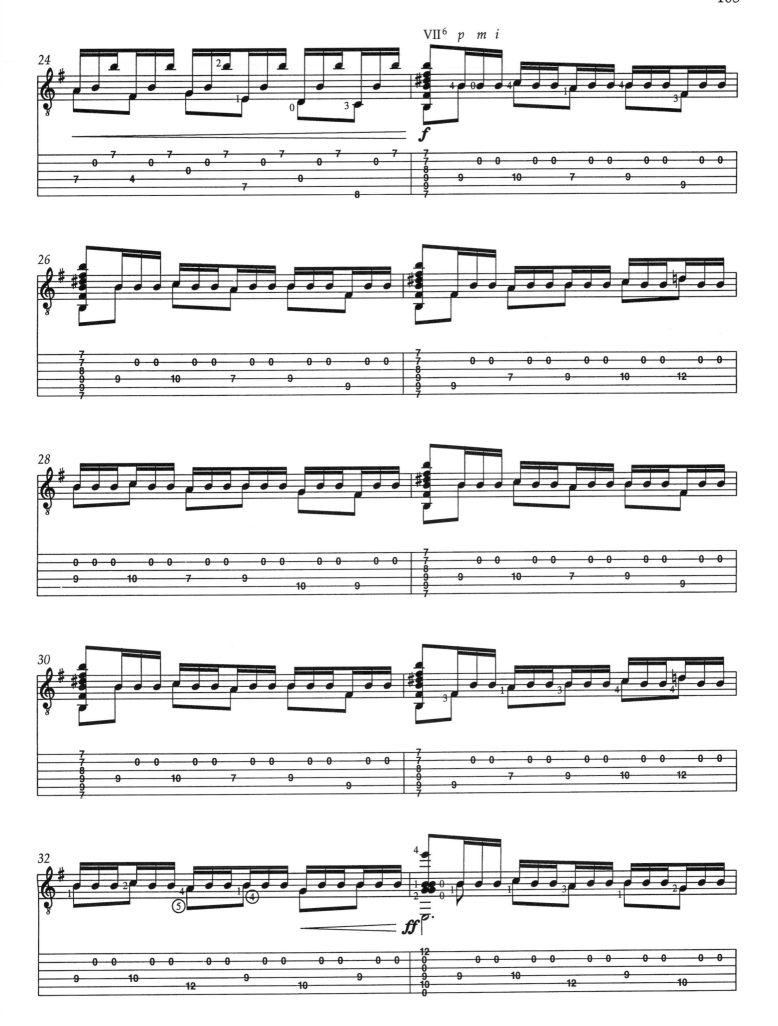

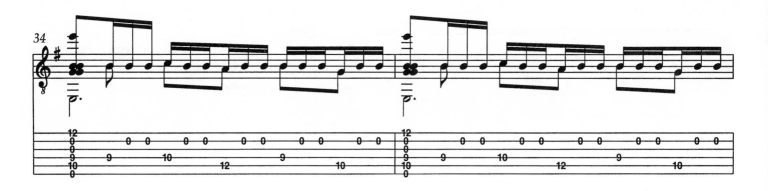

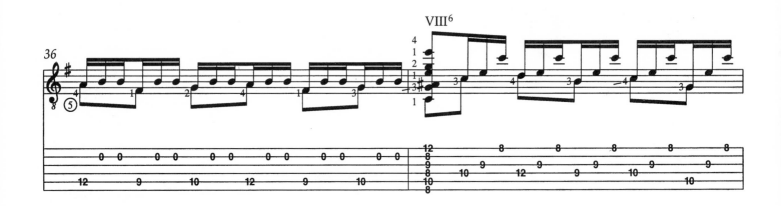

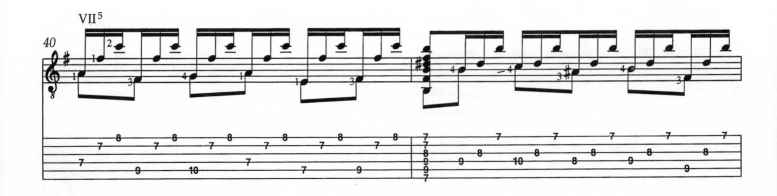

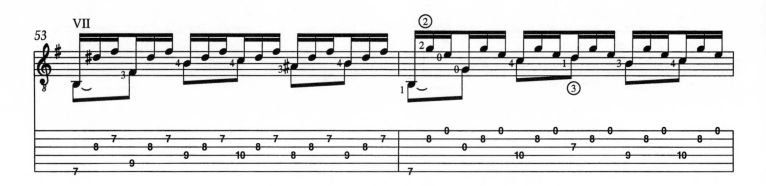

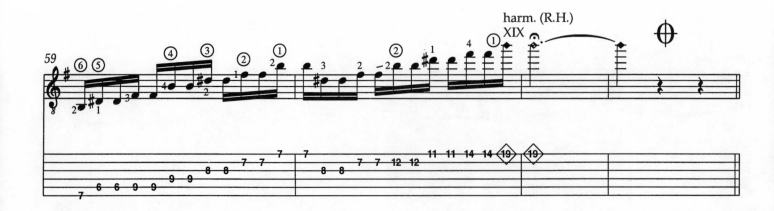

Gnossienne No. 1

from *Trois Gnossiennes*

Erik Satie
(1866–1925)

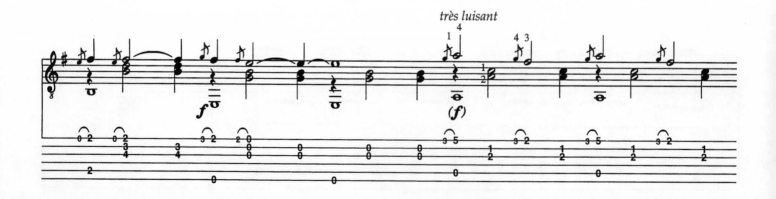

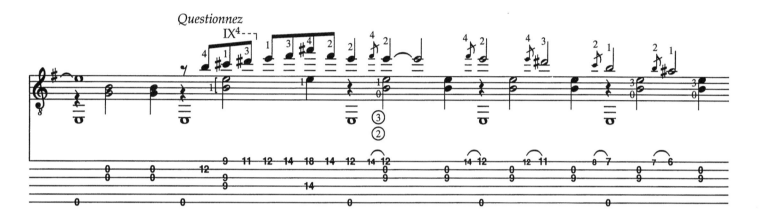

Questionnez

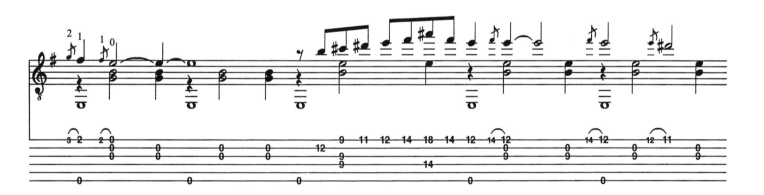

Du bout de la pensée

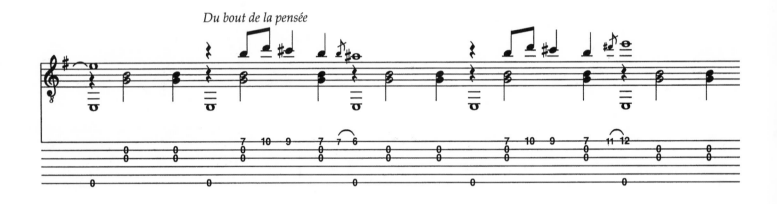

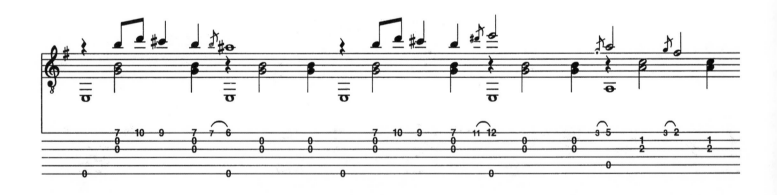

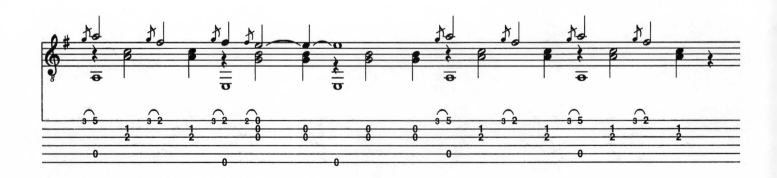

Postulez en vous-même

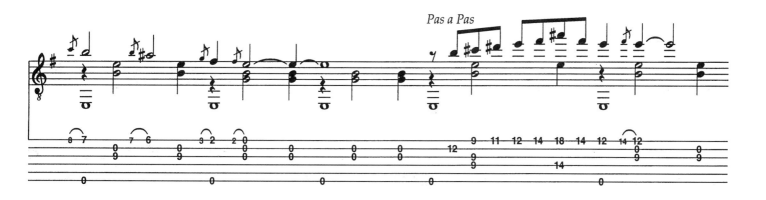

Pas a Pas

Sur la langue

Capricho Árabe

Serenata para Guitarra

Francisco Tárrega
(1852–1909)

END OF EDITION